D0330444

To: _Mrs. Kennon_

From: _Susie_

Date: _12-25-97_

I hope this book uplifts you as much as it has me. Love,
Susie

TIME OUT FOR COFFEE

By

JEANETTE LOCKERBIE

MOODY PRESS

CHICAGO

© 1978 by
THE MOODY BIBLE INSTITUTE
OF CHICAGO

All rights reserved

ISBN: 0-8024-8759-9

21 23 25 27 29 30 28 26 24 22

Printed in the United States of America

To the Ruths in my life—
in appreciation for what you have each taught me
about living and giving.

Contents

7

1

One Thing We Can Never Escape

BIBLE READING: Romans 12:14-19

If it be possible . . . live peaceably (v. 18).

The timeworn saying is that two things we can never escape are death and taxes. I would like to submit that there is one more "inescapable": relationships, or how we get along with other people. You may spend most of your days with just two or three others; you may continually be part of a big group; or, much of your time may be spent alone.

Whichever category you fit will involve getting along. Ask any employer, any employee. Ask yourself, "What one factor more than any other influences the kind of day it will be?" The honest, thoughtful answer will take into account interpersonal relations.

It was my privilege some years ago, while attending English Keswick, to be invited to the Annual Overseas Guests' Tea. Almost all the guests were foreign missionaries, and the brief message was directed toward their interests. I've never forgotten this part of it: the speaker related that he had asked a number of prominent missionaries to share with him their two greatest problems on their particular fields. "Missionary colleagues and the national Christians" was the consensus. "If it were not for these two problems, life would be simple."

Facetious? Perhaps.

Such a life would be robbed not only of meaning but also of challenge. "As much as lies in you, live peaceably," Paul exhorts us. Is that an "out" for not getting along with our associates? As followers of Christ, what "lies in us"? Surely the God-given potential for rightly relating to others.

How do one person's attitudes and actions toward another affect other people?

Think of a day when the company president comes in barking at everybody first thing. "Hm, must have had a fight with his wife," someone says knowingly.

We may have a problem with just one person, but we tend to spray the resultant hostility all over the place, affecting whoever happens to be nearby.

In the light of the importance of our effect on other people, wouldn't it be good to start the day with a prayer something like this?

> Lord, You know what this day will bring and whose life I will touch. Help me to have the right attitudes; help me to want to be a help, and not to create problems.

We can't expect that everyone we meet will have prayed this prayer, or will even have a desire to live peaceably. But we're on top of the situation because (1) we're aware that there can be problems, and (2) we have the assurance that God will help us not to be the one to keep the problems going.

2

What Good Expectations Can Do for You

BIBLE READING: Psalm 62:5-8

According to my earnest expectation (Philippians 1:20).

Marie's job was to circulate with the coffee and sweet rolls cart throughout the plant. It wasn't just the goodies that made her popular; she had a certain look about her; she was a ray of sunshine.

One day a customer remarked to her, "You always look as though you're just expecting something nice to happen."

"I *am,*" Marie replied, cocking her head and smiling.

What a way to live! No wonder she influenced other people for good.

Living with good expectations helps to keep us in a happy frame of mind. It creates excitement for the next minute, the next hour, the next day. I've heard it said that when Mark Twain was asked the secret of his success in life, he answered, "I was born excited."

The Christian life is the most exciting life of all; we never know what pleasant surprise awaits us around the next corner. And expecting good things is saying to God, "I know You have my welfare at heart, Lord." For when we commit our lives totally to the Lord, it's not some kind of cold resignation to the inevitable. Far from it. Such commitment puts us into partnership with the God of the universe, the Author of all creativity. He has a creative program for each of us who wants to get in on it.

Like Marie, I, too, live with happy expectations. Sometimes I can hardly wait to find out what God is going to do next in my life. I find this is such a good, emotionally healthy way to live.

I'm not knocking realism by lauding a spirit of good expectations. Not every experience is for our immediate good. "Nevertheless afterwards," the Bible promises, it will be for our good (Hebrews 12:11).

We all program ourselves according to certain expectations: positive or negative. These are key determiners of our attitudes throughout life.

The pessimist's expectations are gloomy; she perpetually expects the worst. Sadly, this can be as true of the Christian as of her non-Christian colleague. And yet, as believers we have reason to have the greatest of all expectations. David the psalmist knew all about this attitude of mind. He knew where to look when he wrote: "My soul, wait thou only upon God; for my expectation is from him" (Psalm 62:5). David's expectations had the right source for their fulfillment.

Like us, the psalmist knew that it takes both the dark clouds and the sunshine to balance our lives. But we can never know just when God is going to drop a thread of gold into the seeming drabness of our day. Such can be our expectation.

The Bible tells us, "According to your faith be it unto you" (Matthew 9:29). Is it stretching a point to add, "According to your *expectations* be it unto you"?

3

The Part Your Job Plays

BIBLE READING: Philippians 4:6-12

If there be any virtue, . . . think on these things (v. 8*b*).

Among current book titles I noticed one, *Your Job—Survival or Satisfaction.* My reaction was: Must it be either, or? Can't a job provide both survival and satisfaction?

Certainly, between the two, survival would have to take priority. As I pondered that title, I wondered what prevents any job from providing satisfaction. Let me pass on the ideas that came to me.

Looking back is an enemy of present satisfaction. Some women can never feel satisfied because they're dwelling on the past, the "good old days"—when gasoline was cheaper, bus fares lower, taxes less of a burden, and so forth. But such engrossment with other days can't change the present, and it does lead to unhappiness.

Looking to the future is likewise futile if you're depending on the future to give you satisfaction today. "When things get better," we say, as though we have any kind of a guarantee that tomorrow will outdo today in meeting our needs.

14

A discontented spirit militates against satisfaction. The apostle Paul knew this. From his own experience he wrote, "I have learned, in whatsoever state I am, therewith to be content" (Philippians 4:11).

I have *learned*, Paul admitted. Probably "on the job training." He grew to know the peace of a contented spirit, whatever the circumstances of his life.

Looking to the job to do more than can be expected can be still another cause of dissatisfaction. Sometimes we hear people talk about their nine-to-five activity as if that were all there is to life. But after all, that is only a third of the day; we still have a good slice left.

Perhaps the one-third can be survival and the two-thirds satisfaction.

If we look to the job as our *life,* then we will rise and fall emotionally as the work conditions and situations fluctuate. To avoid such a yo-yo existence, we would do well to have meaningful responsibilities and relationships apart from the job.

The great missionary to India, William Carey, had a handle on this problem. As a young man he said, "My business is serving the Lord; I mend shoes to meet expenses." Survival—*and* satisfaction.

4

When They Talk All the Time

BIBLE READING: 1 Thessalonians 4:9-12

Study to be quiet (v. 11).

You will never find it among the courses offered by any college. No credits will be yours for mastering it. But there is a God-mandated subject entitled, "Study to be quiet."

Are you thinking right now, *I know somebody who needs to take that course and practice it?* And in your mind's eye you see a little group of friends trying to have a discussion— but one of the group is monopolizing the conversation.

Some women lose out on fine opportunities because they're known for "talking all the time." They never do the other person the favor of listening, as though in their opinion what is being said is not worthwhile.

Have you ever thought that we *never learn while we're talking?*

Nothing wrong with talking, of course. God made us not only with the ability to communicate with words but also with the desire to do so. It's the *compulsive* talker we're thinking of, the one who "just has to talk."

Some women (and men, too) have this compulsion to

talk. Psychologists would probably explain this as compensating for not being allowed to talk in their early years. They may have been part of a big family and not given much chance to express themselves. There could be a number of reasons. But the average person doesn't stop and consider, Why does so-and-so always have to do the talking? Generally, we come to avoid the continual chatterer.

Another aspect of this subject is that when someone has "studied to be quiet," has deliberately thought of the pros and cons of overtalking, she tends to say something significant when she opens her mouth. I have a beautiful daughter-in-law. She can sit and be intensely interested in the conversation and not have to talk. (I'm trying to learn from her!) But let me say that when Lory speaks, people tend to heed. They know she has something to contribute.

By contrast, how common is this scene: A few people are together, and along comes someone who has a reputation for monopolizing the conversation. "Let's go," someone will say. "Here comes Pat; if we stay, she'll just talk our heads off."

Note, there's no expectation that Pat will have anything to say that could possibly interest them or have value. It could be that she does. But she has earned a name for talking just for the sake of hearing her own voice. This will be hard to change.

Sadly, this is just as true when the compulsive talker is a born-again Christian. People will tend to withdraw from her in self-defense—and she will miss her opportunity of sharing the Good News of the Gospel.

How good it is, then, for us to evaluate ourselves as to whether we need to apply this scriptural injunction, "Study to be quiet." As Christians, we have the added power to do it. God never issues a directive without empowering us to follow it, if we put ourselves in His hands. The Holy Spirit will be our Teacher as we take this course.

5

Validating the Trust

BIBLE READING: Proverbs 3:1-7

So send I you (John 20:21).

Brenda was the most secretive of women. Her associates at work commented to each other, "She doesn't seem to trust a single one of us."

It may be that this woman had good reason from her background not to trust people. Or perhaps the spirit of the age had gotten to her. It's undeniable that there is a paranoia abroad, a general, undefined lack of trust. You've met people afflicted with it. They seem to feel that "Everybody's out to cheat me." And since such prophecies are self-fulfilling, they just might have more such experiences than those of us who are not so suspicious.

Trust begets trust.

The ultimate trust is that the Lord trusts us, even while He bids us trust in Him with all our heart and lean not to our own understanding (Proverbs 3:5). Why the latter? Because at the best, our own judgment is faulty alongside God's, which is based on His omniscience.

Yet Jesus Christ entrusted to us the Gospel, knowing as He does all our potential for failure, discouragement, self-centeredness, and so on. It may seem trite to say that God could have written the message across the skies (and without a trailing of jet vapor). He could have—but He didn't. He wrote it in men's hearts and believed in them that they would get it out to other people.

After nearly two thousand years, with all our weaknesses and failings, we're still concerned about the best means of ringing the world with the Good News.

There's no question that Christ was taking a deliberate chance (from our human point of view) when He didn't set up committees and appoint an ongoing hierarchy to assure that the message would sound throughout the globe. But what if He had listened to such arguments as these:

"How can you trust *Peter,* so fiery and impulsive he'll alienate more people than he will win—and besides, isn't he a proven coward?"

"And John, that dreamer with the gentle manner, he'll never get the job done."

"And take Thomas; you can count on him to get into arguments with his 'You have to show me' attitude."

"Then there's Andrew—but he's such a background figure."

"As for the *women* who believed, well, you can't trust women not to change their minds." And so it might have gone.

Jesus knew all about each individual follower, yet He committed to them the trust of the ages. *He* knew that trust begets trust. He knew, too, that when we trust Him with our whole heart, there's no room for *dis*trust. And believing with our whole heart what He has done for us, we can join the ranks of those He entrusted to spread His Gospel.

Whoever else may have belied our trust, *Jesus* never has; and you and I can likewise validate His trust in us.

6

Coupling Zeal with Caution

BIBLE READING: 1 John 2:4-10

None occasion of stumbling (v. 10)

Elaine works in an aircraft company. Two others in her department are Christians, and together they try to win others to Christ. A special target of their prayer is their supervisor, but she's hard to interest. One day Elaine learned why.

"It's not so much you," the supervisor said to Elaine. "It's some of these others who go around trying to convert everybody. It doesn't seem to occur to them that *they're using the company time,* and that just has to be a form of stealing. I'm not impressed with their religion," she concluded, "in spite of all the tracts and such."

Obviously the well-meant efforts had backfired. No matter that possibly other employees with other interests took time to spread *their* propaganda. The people who complain specifically about Christians witnessing do not tend to be very logical or objective. Nevertheless, we do well to blend common sense and caution with our commendable zeal; otherwise we can give "occasion of stumbling."

A notable soul-winner in our day is Dr. Ralph Byron, chief of surgery at the City of Hope Medical Center in California. In the book *Surgeon of Hope,* Dr. Byron writes,

> The City of Hope has some ninety-two acres. It would be possible for me to go down to the cafeteria or stand on a curb, and proclaim the Gospel! There might be one or two decisions. However, in about twenty-four hours I would be relieved of my position as chief of surgery, and my opportunity to witness to both patients and staff would come to an abrupt end. But, in a less direct approach, it is possible to get the message out in an acceptable fashion. *

The proof that this Christian doctor has found an acceptable approach is that after twenty-two years, he is still known for his untiring witnessing.

Does caution conflict in your mind with Paul's admonition to Timothy to "preach the word . . . in season, out of season" (2 Timothy 4:2)? If so, you may have to rethink, What is *witnessing?* I'm reminded of the saying, "I'd rather see a sermon than hear one any day."

People are not saved by seeing our good works. But it goes without saying that the disenchanted supervisor, and any others whom we may want to lead to Christ, will be all the more likely to listen to our witness if they see us doing a good job each day. We will not then be bucking our own efforts at being effective Christian witnesses.

*Ralph L. Byron, with Jeanette Lockerbie, *Surgeon of Hope* (Old Tappan, N. J.: Revell, 1977), p. 134.

7

The Right Connections

BIBLE READING: Jeremiah 9:23-24; John 1:12

They that know thy name will put their trust in thee
(Psalm 9:10).

Standing in the cafeteria line, Arlene and Sally noticed a
comparative newcomer to the company entering the dining
room with one of the supervisors.

"She seems to be moving up in a hurry," Arlene remarked.
"No doubt she'll make it to the top soon. But *how,* and
why?"

"Oh, come on," Sally responded. "You know as well as I
do that it's all in whom you know. That gal has the right
connections."

Whatever we might think of this, the fact is clearly evident at times. It *is* strategic to know the right people, to
have the right connections. As Jeremiah wrote by inspiration,

Let not the wise man glory in his wisdom, . . .
the mighty . . . in his might, . . .
the rich . . . in his riches:
but let him that glorieth glory in . . . that he . . . knoweth
me [the Lord].

Name-dropping is not generally commendable. But in this instance—when it is the name of Jesus—we can do no better. God has special "promotions"—special honors and favors—for those who ask in the name of His beloved Son, the Lord Jesus Christ. The first is membership in His family (John 1:12). Who would want to pass up such a connection? And from there on, it's up all the way until the final promotion to glory.

Ultimately, it's sheer folly to put our trust in and to glory in anything other than the name of Jesus. But we who know His name wisely put our trust in Him.

We may not be shown special favors; we may not be helped up the ladder two or three steps at a time by whom we know. It may seem a little unfair that someone else is given a promotion that we justly deserve when we don't have the right connections. We may never have a surplus of money or earthly security. Nevertheless, because of whom we know, Jesus Christ, our Lord and Saviour, we are rich with the wealth that can never be taken away from us.

It was no sentimental dreamer who wrote, "I have Christ; what want I more?"

Christ is our connection to God the Father, of whom James writes:

> Every good and every perfect gift is from above, and cometh down from the Father of lights, with whom is no variableness, neither shadow of turning (James 1:17).

Could anything be more beautifully reassuring?
Why settle for a lesser connection?

8

A Bid for Equal Time

BIBLE READING: Malachi 3:14-18

Them that honour me I will honour (1 Samuel 2:30*b*).

It was coffee-break time in the offices of a Christian organization.

"Have you noticed," asked Peggy, "how we seem to have gotten into a rut? Every day we have the same topic of conversation. Do we *have* to talk diets all the time?"

Whether it's the subject of diets (engrossing to many women) or some other interest, a boring sameness can settle on the conversation. That is, unless one person feels there are other areas worthy of discussion, and says so. How we say so is vitally important. For instance, "Haven't we had enough of that topic?" can alienate people so that they will not be disposed to listen to our suggestions of something different.

So how to divert the conversation stream? Here is an approach that generally works. Janice tried it one day when she felt the time could be spent in more worthwhile talk.

"This is changing the subject," she said with a smile, "but

would you like to know about a verse I just found in the Bible? I never saw it till this morning."

Because she didn't put the others down, didn't belittle what they were talking about, they showed a willingness—even eagerness—to hear what she had to share. The "new" verse was:

> Then they that feared the LORD spake often one to another: and the LORD hearkened, and heard it, and a book of remembrance was written before him for them that feared the LORD, and that thought upon his name (Malachi 3:16).

"Think of that!" one of the others exclaimed. "God is so pleased when we talk to each other about Him that He keeps track of it."

"And when we even just *think* about Him, we are remembered," another responded. "That's *wonderful.*"

For that day, at least, the conversation was centered on the most uplifting topic we can ever engage in. But somebody had to start it.

Many times we tend to feel irked or irritated at what goes on around us. Why are we slow to take a creative step to change the situation? When we do, not only will we feel better ourselves, but we can help to contribute something worthwhile to the people with whom we work.

As Christians, no matter where we are, we cannot withdraw from the world and the concerns of those around us; but we can kindly and graciously "take equal time."

9

On the Construction or the Demolition Squad?

BIBLE READING: 1 Thessalonians 5:11-15

Let all things be done unto edifying (1 Corinthians 14:26*b*).

Three office friends stopped on their after-lunch walk to observe a giant bulldozer plowing right through the concrete walls of a building. One of them remarked, "It surely doesn't take as long to knock the thing down as it did to build it."

Truth in a capsule. But who wants to go through life as a knocker down?

Consciously or unconsciously, each of us is daily engaged in being a part of either a construction project or a demolition crew. We are either supplying the components that edify (build), or we are aiding in wrecking.

What, in the round of living, are some of the building blocks we can be conscious of, and mindful to provide, as opportunities come our way?

Appreciation can be as simple as just *noticing* a person rather than treating her as a part of the furniture (as some

27

have complained they're made to feel). Saying "I appreciate you"—not "your work" necessarily, but *"you* as a person"—can change the climate for someone who needs this reassurance from a colleague or superior. Some people go for days without once hearing a word of appreciation that could build them up.

Praise is a companion building-block to appreciation. Nothing will so bring out the best in us as hearing, "You're doing a good job," or, "I'm proud of you," or any *genuine* expression of praise. It's not enough to have such thoughts about a fellow employee; she needs to hear them.

Encouragement is another builder and day-brightener. We all need encouragement to meet what each day brings. Encouragement makes any situation more tolerable; it indicates you *care,* and it's something we can all do to build up each other.

Understanding is a greatly needed building block. One of the ways by which we can gain understanding is by really listening to the other person. No finer compliment than "You understand" can be paid by one person to another.

Christ is the master "Understander." There will be times when it seems no one understands, but Jesus does. He will build us up if we let Him.

Turning from the building blocks, let's take a look at what the wrecking crew accomplishes, and by what means.

Criticism says, "You're not doing it right," or, "How stupid can you be?"—and down the person goes!

Sarcasm in such expressions as "You're great. Everybody should be so fortunate as to have a co-worker like you" uttered in a caustic manner, can do deadly harm to the person's self-esteem. And the damage may never be repaired throughout her life if it has been a constant hammer, hammer, hammer.

Poor expectations are expressed by such words as, "I might have *known* that's what you would do!" "How could I expect anything else from *you?*" Worse than the effect of the bulldozer on a building are such devastating words to a sensitive person. They can totally strip her of self-confidence.

Unfavorable comparisons such as, "You don't do it like Mary [the predecessor] did it"; or, "The woman I worked with on my last job was a lot nicer than you," make a person's self-image hit zero.

Have you seen yourself in these lines? (Hopefully, if you have, it was on the plus side.) Fortunately, as long as we're alive we can change, if we *want* to. With God's help we can rid ourselves of the negatives that knock other people down. We *can* become members of the construction crew.

10

The Fulfillment of the Right Job

BIBLE READING: Matthew 25:14-18

According to his . . . ability (v. 15).

Surely there has to be more to life than this, sighed Ruth as she contemplated another day on her job.

This working woman reflects the feelings of a large percentage who drag themselves, day after day, to a job in which they have little interest. Consequently, they find a minimum of fulfillment and probably do not achieve much success at what they are doing.

In the parable of the talents, it's evident that resources are given according to our ability to use them. As the Distributor of the talents, God knows what abilities He has given each individual.

It makes sense that we will do best the work that coincides with our God-given talents. So it's important that we try to find out what these are. But how to do it?

Along this line, Dr. Clyde Narramore has a saying which is simple and yet profound: "Your natural abilities are God's suggestions for your life's work." If this were heeded, many square pegs would be spared the frustration of being squeezed into round holes!

God has given every one of us some unique ability to do a certain thing or things about which we feel comfortable and competent. It's wise to ask, while we can do something about it, What *is* my particular "thing"? It may be a bent for the technical: business machines and such, a much-in-demand skill; or, it may be skill in the arts: music, painting, writing, or something else, which also has its place. Some people's ability lies in their special way of getting along with other people; the demand will always exceed the supply for such ability.

It can be disastrous for the company, and frustrating to the individual, when the job and the person's natural abilities are poles apart. But it happens. I recall a summer when I had a job in a very large bank. At first I was placed at a machine, but after a few days, lest I wreck too much, I was hastily transferred to a public relations desk. "We think you'll do better with *people*," the personnel manager explained generously. Later—much later, in fact—the Lord made it possible for me to pursue another area of ability He has given me, and for which I will be held accountable one day: writing.

So even if you find yourself in a nonfulfilling position, it's not too late. God will always make it possible for us to do what He has gifted us to do if we really want His will in our lives. We need, then, to discover or uncover our talent(s) and put them to work. And one day we will know the ultimate fulfillment: Christ's "Well done."

11

Praise the Lord, and Dispel the Blues

BIBLE READING: Ephesians 5:17-20

Singing with grace in your hearts (Colossians 3:16).

A customer approached the manager of a Christian bookstore with a rather unusual request. "I'm a professional therapist," the customer explained, "and some of my clients are telling me that what helps them most when they're suffering from depression is to sing snatches of a hymn." The psychologist then proceeded to inquire about certain hymns and where she could find them.

Why should it be strange that singing hymns of praise to our God should calm the mind and dispel severe feelings of dejection?

"I feel uplifted," one client had told her counselor, "when I start to sing instead of dwelling on my bad feelings." If just the act of singing has merit in therapy, how much more can we expect when it is a Christian song? It would be hard to stay downcast when singing, for instance, "Jesus, the Very Thought of Thee" or, "There's Something About That Name," or any one of hundreds of heartwarming, inspiring hymns.

All around us is the evidence that the world at large believes in the efficacy of music to soothe and relax. (Why else do business offices spend the money to pipe it in?) Music is said to provide the right atmosphere for shoppers as well as employees. In addition, all manner of claims are made for what music can do, from allaying the fears of a surgery patient, to causing the cows to give more milk and houseplants to flourish.

David, the sweet singer of Israel, knew the worth of music therapy, and so did the troubled King Saul and his close servants. "David took an harp, and played with his hand: so Saul was refreshed, and was well" (see 1 Samuel 16:14-23).

It's significant that the first song recorded in the Bible was one of victory and praise for deliverance (Exodus 15:1). In the book of Revelation (5:9-13) is the "new song" that inspired the magnificent anthem "Worthy Is the Lamb." This, too, is a song of deliverance and redemption and praise and worship to Jesus Christ, our Lord and Saviour.

Are you depressed? Try singing with grace in your heart unto the Lord. It works!

12

Not What We Do, But How We Do It

BIBLE READING: 1 Corinthians 13:1-4

Her ways are ways of pleasantness (Proverbs 3:17).

Phyllis sensed that her colleagues didn't really like her, and she couldn't understand why. She had a genuine love for people and saw herself as helpful in a number of ways. One day she determined to find out why she was unpopular.

She had one close friend, Grace; she approached her and asked, "Why don't the others like me? What do I do that nobody wants to be friends with me?"

"It's not exactly what you do or don't do, Phyllis, it's—" Grace hesitated.

"Go on, go on," Phyllis urged. "I can take it."

"Well—oh, it's such a little thing, and I'm sure you're not aware it hurts them." Grace shifted from foot to foot, uncomfortable at being in the situation. Then she blurted out, "You go around correcting people's grammar all the time."

"What! You mean that's why they try to shun me!" Phyllis looked incredulous. "Why, all I'm trying to do is *help* them."

"It's not what you say, it's how you do it. It's a put-down to have you come along and pick up a fragment of conversation, then publicly sort it out as though it were letters on a Scrabble board. You cause people to feel ignorant and uneducated just because you want everybody else to be as precise as you are about every single word. There, now I've told you." Grace sighed in relief.

Obviously Grace has more insight than Phyllis into human nature.

Criticism is always hard to take, and nobody likes to be corrected in public. Does this mean that we should never try to help when we see an area in which we can be helpful? No! As Christians we have a God-given mandate to be helpful to each other. But there's a time and a place and a way to do it, and the other person's feelings must be taken into consideration.

Many a woman has advanced because someone cared enough to help her. The motive and intent of the helper are what make the difference. If we correct a person because of our own intolerance of an error, that's one thing. If, however, we think, *I'd like to help that woman,* then we find the most loving and nonthreatening way to offer our help *without being patronizing.* In this way we gain a friend; we don't lose one.

Love suffers long—and is kind.

13

One, Two, Three Steps to Deterioration

BIBLE READING: Psalm 1

Those . . . who do not hang around with sinners
(v. 1, TLB).

David might have been writing about our day when he
outlined in three precise steps the gradual process that subtly
destroys the once witnessing Christian: walking—standing—sitting.

Take Sara: Around her church family, she had been
known as an enthusiastic, radiant Christian. And it was
true. Then she went to work for a secular organization, and
in six months she was a totally different person. From being
the happy inspiration of her pastor and church friends, she
became cold and indifferent. It didn't happen all at once;
her lack of attendance at prayer meeting was the first indication. Her new associates at work had said with raised
eyebrows, "Prayer meeting! I thought that had gone out
with hoop skirts," and Sara felt funny about ever mentioning
it again.

Next it was the group Bible study. Her workmates didn't
make fun of that; they invited her to join them in a cul-

tural group that met the same night. Going with them spelled acceptance by them, so Sara went, and she began to go regularly.

It was a short step, then, to missing Sunday school and church once in a while. "It's the only day that you have to do what you please," a fellow employee explained to her. (What had happened to *Saturday?* we might ask.) And gradually, Sara salved her conscience by her ungodly friends' rationale as she skipped church altogether.

Her actions in regard to church were just the outward indication that she was changing. The real damage was being done on the inside. (We need to keep in mind, though, that we never backslide *alone;* no matter how insignificant we might feel our Christian testimony to be, someone is sure to be taking us as his example.) Sara's appetite for Bible study had diminished. She could not enjoy communication with God in prayer, for the Holy Spirit is too faithful to let us be happy in God's presence when our hearts are far from Him.

Undernourished through her lack of prayer and Bible study, she became spiritually puny and increasingly unable to do anything but stand where her associates stood, and sit where they sat (both figuratively and literally).

Perhaps from sheer familiarity with the first psalm, we fail to see its message as being relevant to us today. We quote it; we memorize it; we sing it to lovely tunes (At least if you're Scottish like me, you sing it.) But David's first psalm is more than inspiration; it is a solemn warning. We can be like a tree, with its many benefits to mankind, or we can be like chaff, for which no one has any use. It all depends on where and with whom we walk—and stand—and sit.

Backsliding is a creeping menace against which we can successfully war only as we delight ourselves in the Lord and meditate on His Word.

14

Gratitude, an Attitude

BIBLE READING: 1 Thessalonians 5:14-24

It is a good thing to give thanks unto the LORD (Psalm 92:1).

Quite frequently these days we're hearing a spontaneous "Praise the Lord!"

What does this do to you when you hear it? Perhaps you view the person speaking as overly pious, as somewhat saccharin. Or do you suspect that she may be more talk than Christian walk?

Some view the exuberant, vocal "Praise the Lord" individual as out of it, not sensitive to what's going on in the world around him (that calls for anything *but* praising the Lord!). Others view them as strictly Pollyanna.

We are all entitled to our opinions. For myself, I would have to confess that I did not always have a consciousness of what it meant to be truly thankful to God; no one would ever have thought I was overdoing the praise. But in the past few years God has been teaching me, among other valuable lessons, the worth of a thankful spirit.

"In every thing give thanks," the Bible exhorts (1 Thessalonians 5:18). *Everything?* You can't mean it seriously, Paul. Not everything.

Yes, everything. I even came across a verse that says we should be thankful *for* all things (Ephesians 5:20)—and that's much more difficult to do consistently. But I'm finding that it pays.

Actually, obedience is often its own reward. God says, "Be thankful," so we can expect to profit more from obeying that injunction than from disregarding it, whatever we might think of it. God would never be guilty of issuing an edict that is impossible for us to obey.

Be thankful for a stuck elevator that means we walk countless steps?

Be thankful for a moody colleague, the kind you never know how to take?

Be thankful for a demanding boss you can never quite satisfy?

Be thankful for a headache?

What about a major loss, something that shatters your life?

Little things. Big things. In everything give thanks. We would be less than human if at times we didn't question, How *can* I be thankful?

I can only share with you what I'm learning in God's school. Saying, "Thank You, God," is our acknowledgment that He is sovereign in our lives. It's saying, in effect, "Lord, I don't know, and I don't understand what You're doing in my life. But I know You love me, You *care,* and You know what the future holds for me."

It's interesting that we are instructed to pray, "Give us *this day* our *daily* bread." The God who takes care of us by

40

the day is willing and able to guide us through whatever circumstances He sees fit to route us.

So we can confidently trust Him and thank Him for all things—at all times. Gradually we will find gratitude to be a fixed attitude. When we cultivate this spirit of thankfulness, we will keep findings things to be thankful for all day long. This habitual attitude lightens and brightens the day.

15

It Didn't Seem Important

BIBLE READING: ACTS 26:13-18

I am sending you, to open their eyes (vv. 17-18, NASB).

Alice was new on the job, and at the first coffee break she shared in a simple, direct manner what Jesus meant in her life. To her amazement, Joan, one of her new colleagues, eagerly, almost hungrily, asked Alice to tell her more, and within a few days she had accepted Jesus as her Saviour.

As the two got to know each other, Alice asked Joan if she had ever known other Christians. "Oh, yes, there were quite a few at the last place I worked," Joan answered. "I would hear them talking about their Christian activities—meetings and such—"

Alice interrupted, with a puzzled look on her face. "How is it, then, that you grabbed at what I was saying as though you'd never heard it and as if that was your one and only chance?"

"It *was* the first time I ever heard," Joan insisted. Then, in a wistful tone, she added, "It seemed that what those other Christians believed wasn't *important enough* to them that they should share it with me."

Granted, Joan's may be a somewhat isolated case. Nevertheless, shouldn't it cause us to question: Am I hugging my salvation to myself? Do I act as though Christians were a secret society ("for believers only")?

Or am I a witness? Is my salvation so important to me that I just have to share it with others?

What to share seems to be a problem with some well-intentioned Christians. Here we can do no better than to emulate Paul. Tell what happened when you were saved. Isn't this what a witness does, anyway? Nothing is more effective than saying, "This is what happened." You're sure of a listener. So you didn't have a flashing-lights-and-voices-from-heaven experience like Paul. But if you had a genuine encounter with the living Christ, you and I can say,

> Something happened when He saved me;
> Happened in my heart.

Nothing in all the world is so important as that!

And if we really believe the Bible—that without Christ those people we associate with every day are lost, lost, *lost*—how can we keep from being witnesses?

16

Being a Name—Not a Number

BIBLE READING: John 10:1-14

The Lord knows those who are His (2 Timothy 2:19, NASB).

Standing in the cafeteria line, Joan and Marie noticed the president of the company come along, talk to one of the employees, and make his way out of the cafeteria again.

"Hm!" Joan whispered to Marie. "Must have been one of the five thousand of us he knows."

"Well, you know who *he* is," Marie responded.

"A lot of good that does me. Sure I know him, but he wouldn't know me from a hole in the wall," countered Joan.

This is a common enough situation. There are certain prominent people we say we "know" (we may have heard them speak sometime, or have been at the same large function they attended), but 99 percent of the time they might not even know we exist.

Jesus is not like that.

Likening us to sheep—for purposes of illustration only—Jesus tells us that He knows us by our *name*. It's always an ego-building experience to be called by name; it makes us feel we're important to the person who is speaking. It says,

"I know you are there—*you,* not just a member of a group, but you as an individual."

In a day when to an alarming and dehumanizing degree we are becoming nothing but a number, how comforting to realize that God knows our names. When I came to Jesus and asked Him to forgive my sin and take me into His family, He didn't say, "Come in. You are Believer No. 71,342,009." No. He knows my name is Jeanette as surely as He knows His mother's name is Mary.

How do we know Him?

In the parable, the distinguishing feature of the shepherd is His voice. Many shepherds call their sheep. But sheep recognize just one voice—"and a stranger will they not follow" (John 10:5).

A myriad of voices bombard us, some of them tempting us away from the Lord. How do we recognize the voice of the One who is calling us by name? As we spend time in God's Word, as we commune with Him in prayer, we become sensitive to the voice of the Good Shepherd. One thing is certain: if the voice is saying what is contrary to the revealed will of God, *it is not His voice.* It takes keen discernment to listen to and obey only the voice of God. He will never know *us* better than He does today. But we can grow and learn more of Him. The more we know about God, the more we will feel like a person and not a number.

17

A Time Not to Say "Cheer Up"

BIBLE READING: Ecclesiastes 3:1-7

To everything there is a season (v. 1).

Around the coffee machine, three or four women were discussing one of the current books on mental health. In particular, they were talking about how Christians in general act toward one another and of the importance of being sensitive to another's moods.

Later that day, one of the group returned to her office to find a little note from a co-worker who had been involved in the discussion. The words were few—and right on target. They were: "Thanks for not using the 'Cheer up!' tactics on me the past few weeks."

What was the writer of the note saying between the lines?

"I've been rather downhearted for a little while. You didn't pry or probe into the reason; you didn't say, 'What's eating you?' or, 'Don't you know that a Christian can always find something to rejoice in?' or anything like that. You treated me in a normal manner. Now that I'm myself again, I want you to know that I appreciate your leaving me alone, not coming at me with, 'Cheer up! Things could be worse, you know.'"

How do I know what she really meant? I know because I am the one who found the note on my desk. By that time, the lady wanted to talk, to share what she had been going through. First, though, she wanted to make it clear that any "cheer up" approach would have been lost on her, would not have helped her one bit at the time.

I'm trying to remember that lesson. Because I have a genuine love for this woman, and consequently an interest in how she's feeling, the Lord must have given me a special awareness and sensitivity toward her needs. It was reassuring, then, to get the affirmation that this is indeed an effective way to be a good friend at certain times.

The wise Solomon was aware that there is a time for everything: a time to share, and a time to be allowed *not* to share what we are feeling deeply.

When we demonstrate this sensitivity toward another person at such times, it comes across to him as "She doesn't know, but she *cares*." Only God, by His Holy Spirit at work in our lives, can give us this kind of loving awareness that to everything there is a season, and the wisdom to speak or to be silent as best fits the need.

Wouldn't this be a good thing to pray for each morning before we go out to mingle with people all day long?

18

The Christian and Ethics

BIBLE READING: Matthew 6:31-34

Render to all what is due them (Romans 13:7, NASB).

It costs to "seek . . . first the kingdom of God, and his righteousness" (Matthew 6:33). This is especially true in the area of ethics in business. For instance, a fellow employee complains that you're "overdoing it"; she urges you to slow down or be less efficient, because your diligence is reflecting on the other employees.

What do you do? Become an indifferent worker, not caring how much you accomplish of that which is expected of you?

Take another case. Your employer is demanding that you do a certain thing that will cheat the customer. How do you handle it?

As Christians, we have the biblical edict that we "owe no man any thing but . . . love" (Romans 13:8). This applies to all men, whether the boss or the client or the customer.

I confess that I had not heard much preaching along this line, and it had not been brought home to me personally

48

(though I would hope I have been, and am, ethical in my practices).

Sometimes we can learn from the single-eyed new convert. This happened to me when I was in Hong Kong. I met people to whom ethics in business was a priority in their new faith. One of these was Lee, who works in a wig factory there. One day the owner came and told her that she must begin to reduce by several thousands the hairs in each wig she made. But Lee didn't feel that this was right, and she decided she could not go along with it, since the customers would be assuming that the product was unchanged. But jobs were scarce. What would she do if she lost this job? She prayed, and a few hours later she approached her employer. After showing proper Oriental respect, she explained that she could not carry out his new orders. Then, before he could react and perhaps fire her, she added, "Here is something I *will* do. So that you will not lose money, I am willing to work for you two extra hours each day *without pay.*"

Totally taken aback, the employer sent her back to her work. Later that day he came and told her that he could not accept her sacrifice of two hours and that she could continue making the wigs the same as before.

This young Christian had opted for Christ and His righteousness, and the Lord had kept His promise about "these things."

We may not always see such a resolution of our situation, but *it will always be right to do right,* and ultimately God will vindicate us and add the needed things in our lives.

19

Having a Plan of Action

BIBLE READING: Luke 1:1-4

Let all things be done decently and in order (1 Corinthians 14:40).

Do you sometimes arrive at your place of business, glance over the pile of work, and sigh, not quite sure where to begin? Do you secretly envy the person who seems so efficient, who accomplishes so much more than you do in the same amount of time?

Yet, everything else being equal, there is usually a simple explanation. I admit that I'm not the most orderly of persons on the job. I tend to rationalize by saying, "It's not where it belongs, but I *know* where it is!" (I wouldn't, however, recommend this kind of filing system.) Even though I generally can put my hand on something when I need it, I know, too, that organization will defeat disorganization every time.

God is for *order;* He is not for *confusion.* This is taught in the Scriptures (see 1 Corinthians 14:33), and it is demonstrated in all of His creation.

Doing things in order is good stewardship of our time.

Another way to "redeem the time" is to work with a plan. Rather than sighing over where to begin, I've learned to tackle things in order by making a simple list. We don't have to create an elaborate chart, but it does help when we have a "Things to Do Today" schedule. And what a sense of accomplishment when we can tick off the "done" items! The list accomplishes two things: it keeps before us the priority responsibilities, and it can prevent us from being sidetracked.

There will always be the temptation to yield to what has come to be known as "The Tyranny of the Urgent," those interruptions that steal away the minutes and the hours, leaving the really important things undone. Consequently, at the end of the day we're both tired and frustrated, rather than having the good, healthy, ego-building feeling, "I've done a good job today."

It's significant that we never read of the Lord Jesus that He was in a hurry. He knew what He had to do, and He did it. Knowing what was important, He was not swayed and sidetracked from His purpose by the seemingly urgent. At the end of His earthly life, He could say, "I have finished the work which thou gavest me to do" (John 17:4).

God has a plan for you and me, a work for *us* to finish; we will accomplish all the more if we have a plan of action and stick with it, despite what others might urge us to do.

20

You Don't Have to Be Your Own Worst Enemy

BIBLE READING: Proverbs 18:12-16, 24

A man that hath friends must shew himself friendly (v. 24).

Julie and Marge watched as a member of their stewardess team swaggered past them toward the ramp.

"She could probably be a nice girl," commented Julie.

"Right," agreed Marge, "that is, if she wasn't busy being her own worst enemy."

Would anyone deliberately set out to be her own enemy? Yet it does happen.

In order to look at how not to alienate people around us, it might be best to consider how to become our own best friends.

I've heard that someone in training to spot counterfeit currency never studies the counterfeit. He concentrates on the authentic, memorizing every facet of it. By thorough familiarization with the genuine, he readily discerns the false.

In like manner, we can study acceptable behavior to the

degree that the unacceptable is easily recognized. We can even progress until we discern this in ourselves; a great step toward maturity!

One method is to ask ourselves, What do I especially like and appreciate in my friends or acquaintances? Think about *specific* traits. Then probe further: Am I like that? Could someone say the same about me?

This can be followed by: What, in other people, turns me off, irks me, causes me not to want to be with them very much? It's not always easy to pinpoint such things. We often say, "There's something about her—I don't know, I just can't like her." But some "unlikables" are readily spotted.

Why is it important that we be likable?

One reason is that we will be happier, for almost certainly if others are not liking us, we're not liking ourselves. Another reason is that, as Christians, we should do everything we can to be an influence for God wherever we are. And it's difficult to influence positively someone who doesn't like us; they will not listen to our witness.

I've met people who sluff the whole thing off with, "That's the way I am; if they don't like me, that's too bad." It *is* too bad, for such a defense bristles with hostility. It's not a happy person speaking. God wants us to grow in grace, to move on in Christ toward being a little more like Him. As we do so honestly, we can't help but become more likable.

And this is the very antithesis of being your own worst enemy.

21

C for Cancel

BIBLE READING: Isaiah 44:21-24

I am he that blotteth out thy transgressions (Isaiah 43:25).

As a new Christian, I was introduced to many new songs. One chorus we sang went something like this:

> God has blotted them out;
> I'm happy and glad and free.

My mind reverted to that joyful thought when, not long ago, I was initiated into some of the wonders of the computer world. With no interest in computers nor any desire to understand their intricacies, I had just sat in on a training session for those who would be operating the equipment (I like to learn new words, and computerese is a new *language,* or so I had been told.)

"Default messages"—"Motivation code." The meaningless (to me) phrases swirled around, going in one ear and out the other, until something the expert was explaining caused my interest to perk up. I found myself listening intently. "If you don't like a line you've done, just enter a *C* for cancel."

Canceled. As if it had not been programmed in.

Blotted out. As if it had never been.

What an analogy, I reasoned, glad now that I had come to learn computerese. To my mind came the words of the Lord Jesus, "Now ye are clean" (John 15:3). Not through a keypunched *c,* not through the application of a chalkboard eraser, but "through the word which I have spoken," the Saviour said. And He *is* the Word.

And that is where the analogy breaks down.

It's God the Son who redeemed us by "blotting out the handwriting of ordinances that was against us . . . nailing it to his cross" (Colossians 2:14). That's *canceling* it! And with Him there is no possibility for errors, no chance that the operator will inadvertently punch something other than *C* for cancel.

The computer is indisputably marvelous. But have you thought that it is so only because it is the product of man's (*God-given*) brain? For the God who threw the stars into place, who stretched out the skies, the most sophisticated computer is like a do-it-yourself toy.

And only God can cancel sin. His *C* is Christ Jesus, who came into the world to save sinners.

22

My Favorite Verse Tells Me

BIBLE READING: Ephesians 1:1-7

I have chosen you (John 15:16).

My favorite Bible verse is the very first verse that had meaning for me as a Christian.

It was the morning following my conversion experience. My new Christian friends advised me to begin reading the Bible each morning (one of them gave me her own Bible for starters!). With no instruction as to where I should begin, I just opened my new Bible and—up popped these words: "Ye have not chosen me, but I have chosen you."

So amazed was I at the sheer truth of the statement that I stopped right there and said, "That's *true,* God! I was not seeking You when You reached out to me." My first conversation with the Lord.

It was as I became an avid reader of the Bible that I came again to "my" verse, and learned how very much more it held for me (and you):

> Ye have not chosen me, but I have chosen you, and ordained you, that ye should go and bring forth fruit, and that your fruit should remain.

Chosen by the God of heaven. Isn't that enough to make any woman feel special!

And for a *purpose*: God had a plan for my life when He chose me.

According to God's plan, *my work for Him would be lasting.*

In God's good time He revealed to me that His ultimate work for me was in the field of Christian writing and in teaching others to write. And what a joy this is, for what is more lasting than the printed word?

Then one day as I was sharing this verse with a seminar group in Indonesia, God blessed me with a new insight into its meaning. It was this: God expects me to produce fruit for Him; then, reasonably, He has implanted the particular kind of "ability seed" necessary for me to produce what He expects. Fair enough? And this is a great comfort if, like me, you're rather limited in your abilities.

Everyone has some seeds of ability. All that God requires of us is that we nurture them and produce according to what He has put within us. There are various areas of ability, for example:

> respons-ibility   flex-ibility
> avail-ability   depend-ability
>   account-ability

Think what these traits mean in the everyday world, how they affect relationships on the job.

Likewise, there is a variety of seeds which God implants; there are *kindness* seeds, *friendship* seeds, *generosity* seeds, *sharing* and *caring* seeds.

God needs all kinds of fruit producers. He has chosen

you and He has chosen me that we might bring forth fruit, and that it should remain.

As if to confirm for us that He has chosen us, God's Word says that He chose us "before the foundation of the world" (Ephesians 1:4). Even way back then, God had a purpose for your life and mine, and *today* is a vital part of it.

23

Escaping the Mold

BIBLE READING: Ephesians 4:23-27

Transformed by the renewing of your mind
(Romans 12:2).

"Can You Escape the Mold?" was the title of a filler ar-
ticle in *Modern Secretary* some time ago. The answer comes
right out of the Bible: "Be not conformed to this world,"
or, as *The Living Bible* paraphrases Romans 12:2,

> Don't copy the behavior and customs of this world,
> but be a new and different person with a fresh new-
> ness in all you do and think.

The secret of all this fresh newness that is so appealing to
others and invigorating to you is wrapped up in Paul's admonition. It's significant that, having committed yourself
wholly to God, the first area of renewal is your *mind*. This
gives the lie to the host of critics of Christianity who view
it as a mindless religion. They couldn't be more wrong.

What is it that makes us strike out in a new and different direction at conversion and commitment to Christ. It's
our *changed mind*, as well as our new heart.

"I've changed my mind" almost always presages a change

of plans and activities. It results in something that shows on the outside.

What form will the transformation take? The same form as conforming to the world; it will be demonstrated in conversation, appearance, priorities, behavior toward others around us, values in general. All of these will reveal whether we have indeed escaped the world's mold.

In your work situation you may be the only one who has escaped the world's mold. This places you in a strategic position. You are one of a kind. But you can change that! By a consistent Christian life, by a loving and cooperative attitude, by prayer, and by a clear witness of what Christ means to you in your daily life, you may win over someone with whom you work. There was never a day when so many people were disenchanted with the things they've tried to find satisfaction and some kind of peace of heart. They may not know these lines, but they know the inner gnawing:

> I've tried the broken cisterns, Lord,
> But oh, their waters failed.

If you're a lone Christian, perhaps someone near you is just waiting for you to share. She wants to escape her mold.

Then there will be two of you.

24

Saints—They're Hard to Live With

BIBLE READING: Matthew 23:1-7

Do not sound a trumpet before thee (Matthew 6:2).

One of the sights and sounds I remember from a trip to Jerusalem is the long-robed men praying audibly and ostentatiously. It was of such attention-seeking religionists that the Lord Jesus used the metaphor of sounding a trumpet before you.

"Holier than thou" is our term today. Such people, however dedicated they might genuinely be, irk the rest of us.

Madge tended to be this kind of person. She had an irritating habit of implying (if she didn't always come right out and say it), *"I've* read my chapter in the Bible this morning, have *you?"* The veiled insinuation was that her fellow Christians on the job were not as diligent in their devotions as she. All this did was turn the others off. Madge just alienated people around her by her show of hyperholiness.

It's sad that usually we don't know to what extent we're having a negative effect on other people by our intent to demonstrate what good Christians we are. We would all refrain from acting like "saints" if we realized we were guilty of such practices.

Naturally we're not referring to spontaneous sharing of our blessings, or of encouraging one another in our Christian walk. Rather, we're deploring the smug superiority we see in some believers. This can be a put-down to a sensitive soul.

But how can we, as Christians, know when we are being even slightly obnoxious?

Generally we are not favored in having an honest friend or two who will dare our possible affront or anger by telling us what we're doing to other people. When we do have such a friend (I have a couple), it pays to listen when they constructively criticize what we're doing or saying. I don't mean the "friend" who is a congenital nitpicker, who can see great flaws in whatever we do. But there are a few genuine friends who will—if we let them—clue us in for our own good, and the good of those around us.

It's of such people that my countryman, Robert Burns, wrote:

O wad [would] some power the giftie gie [give] us,
To see oorselves as ithers see us.

Then, enlightened and acting on the new insights, we would be Christians *who are easy to live with.*

25

Motivated by Trust

BIBLE READING: Matthew 10:5-10; 28-31

Greater works than these shall he do (John 14:12).

It must have been a great day for the chosen twelve. One phase of their training over, they were being sent out on the road. Their instructions were explicit, what to do and what not to do. The master Teacher combined *realism*—they would encounter rejection—and *encouragement*. They would not be alone, for the Spirit of the Father would accompany them. Add to that Christ's assurance to them of their *personal value* to God, His trust in them, and they were ready for the task!

Employers can learn a lot from Christ's confidence in His followers. They were human; they had weaknesses as well as strengths. Knowing all about them, Jesus trusted them with great responsibility—and they rose to the challenge.

How often, by contrast, does the employer (Christian as well as non-Christian) impose the responsibility but deny the authority or the trust that should accompany it.

Marie, for example, complained justifiably. "She [the boss] loads responsibility on me, then she acts as though she can't trust me to do things right. She stands over me, giving me the feeling that she thinks I'll flub."

What does it do for us when we're given a position of trust on the job? Generally, when it's a task we're competent at, responsible for, and being trusted to carry out, it brings out the very best in us. We strive to prove worthy of the trust placed in us. We aim to do greater things. We become even more responsible, more dependable.

But when the responsibility does not carry the corresponding trust and the authority to fulfill it, such responsibility is a mockery.

It's a wise superior who will let an employee prove herself, even if at first she may need guidance and help in decision making. There's no better way to foster confidence in a person.

Jesus had thoroughly trained very ordinary men. He then commissioned them and expected that they would succeed. How much, we might ponder, did their phenomenal success have to do with their Master's good expectations of them? "Greater things will you do," He had assured them. And they did!

Our Lord was too wise to delegate responsibility and withhold trust.

26

How's the Climate?

BIBLE READING: Psalm 42:5-11

Be ye stedfast, unmoveable (1 Corinthians 15:58).

When asked, "What do you find to be a source of hindrance to good feelings among your staff?" an executive answered, *"Moodiness:* people who are unpredictable—up one day and down the other—and nobody knows how to take them."

Probably, as employees, most of us feel the same. It's hard to live with moodiness. One person's seesaw emotions can affect the total emotional climate at work.

Why is moodiness a luxury most of us cannot afford if we hope to have reasonably good relationships with our fellow workers?

One reason is that no one owes it to us to study our "mood of the day" and adjust his behavior toward us accordingly. That's too much to expect. Nor does anyone appreciate having to figuratively walk on eggs around the moody individual.

What causes moodiness, and how can the moody Christian deal with this problem (assuming she wants to)?

Moodiness can reflect that the person has never grown up; it's a mark of immaturity when such a person doesn't realize she is imposing a burden on those around her. Also, moodiness can be an effort (conscious or unconscious) to gain attention. A very insecure woman might project mood swings just to get someone to notice her.

It's only fair to say that every one of us has *some* days when she feels more on top than others. We may even have times when we feel our spirits have hit bottom. But, as believers, we have God's resources. Even David the psalmist had his emotional ups and downs, but he knew where to go for help at such times.

"Why art thou cast down, O my soul?" he asked, and then replied to himself, "Hope thou in God," and "Therefore will I remember thee" (Psalm 42:5-6). A solid resource for upping our spirits is remembering how God has always kept His word and met our needs as we've called on Him. In another place, David stated, "My help cometh from the LORD" (Psalm 121:2). And David had no corner on all this help from the Lord.

We *will* have up days and down days, for a variety of reasons. But we, too, can hope in God and reverse our own emotional climate.* In turn, we will be able to reflect on a practical level that being a Christian works for us in our daily living. We will not, then, impose our moods on our colleagues, upsetting the climate and hindering good relationships.

By His Spirit, God will enable us to be steadfast and unmovable.

*NOTE: The author does not purport to be diagnosing or prescribing for anyone who may be suffering from severe disturbances; such cases call for professional help.

27

A Way of Escape

BIBLE READING: 1 Corinthians 10:10-13

I can do all things through Christ (Philippians 4:13).

Temptation comes in many ways, and in the workaday world it is most difficult to handle when it involves other people. Perhaps I can best illustrate this through an experience of my own.

I arrived at my office all agog over a particular project I was working on. My secretary and I had gone over what each of us would do to assure that the deadline would be met. To my dismay, another staff member had taken over the secretary and given her another assignment. I was *furious,* not just for myself but for the piece of work which would thus be delayed when we could ill afford to have it late.

My bubbly eagerness, even my creativity, hit zero.

My first impulse was to complain vocally. But I know the potential for spouting off under emotional stress. So I wrote out the situation as I saw it and as it affected my work—and my relationships with two other people. I headed for the proper authority to present my little statement. He was on the phone, so I left. On the way back to my office, though still sort of seething, I was beginning to be more sensible. Even so, a second time I ventured with my complaint, and again, it aborted. This time, I began to ask the Lord if He was telling me something. And He was.

It's not wrong to have feelings that there has been an injustice, or whatever, when the situation brings on these feelings. But there's a right way to handle them. Looking back, I can see where so many negative things would have come out of my impulsive response. As it was, because the Lord protected me from forging ahead, the situation resolved itself within a couple of hours.

As I see it, because I do "commit my way to the Lord" before I step out of the door each morning, God is faithful. He would not let me "blow it" that morning. He made a way of escape. Satan would have had a field day all that day as one thing would surely have led to another. But if we will let Him, God will always provide a way of escape. He will empower us for "all things." And one of these "all things" that is most difficult for most of us is being quiet when in ourselves we would spout off and thereby do harm.

Admittedly, I've been a slow learner in this area of Christian living. But God is patient with me. Here is another lesson He has taught me. Before reacting to frustrating and irritating situations, I've learned to ask myself:

If I do this (impulsive "setting things right"), will I be glad tomorrow—a week from now, a year from now—that I took this action? Or will I cringe and hang my head at the very thought that I could behave so?

It is for times of stress in every area of life that we have

Christ's wonderfully assuring promise that *He* will strengthen us for "all things."

And He does make a way of escape that we *can* have victory in the situation that would otherwise defeat us.

28

You Would Understand

BIBLE READING: 1 Kings 3:5-13

Give . . . thy servant an understanding heart (v. 9).

Two friends, Anne and Maria, were discussing a certain thing Anne had dreamed of buying for a long time.

"I do hope you'll be able to get it soon," Maria said. "I know it'll mean so much to you."

With a warm smile, Anne replied, "You would understand that."

What was Anne saying? That her friend was more understanding about things in general? Not necessarily. I think she meant, "You know my interests; you're interested in me to the point of realizing what gives me real pleasure."

How do we acquire this brand of understanding?

Where does it spring from?

Is it a quality that can be cultivated?

How much demand is there for such understanding?

To the first of these questions we can answer that this brand of understanding comes largely by listening. Listening produces the innate sense that makes people say when they receive a gift from us, "How did you know that it's *exactly* what I wanted?"

We all know people who are by no means beauty queens; they are not super intellectuals, not especially creative. But they have that something about them that makes other people say, "She understands."

Perhaps if we recognized the worth of this quality more than we do, some of us might be praying Solomon's prayer.

Solomon didn't have a corner on God-given understanding. He did exhibit superior wisdom in that the one thing he asked for, *knowing that whatever he asked, would assuredly be given,* was an understanding heart.

God will still graciously give an understanding heart to any of us who wants this gift to use for His glory. And surely nothing can better smooth relationships than true understanding. How often, in sheer frustration, someone who needs help will lament, "You just *don't* understand."

Having asked God for this priceless gift, we then set about to use it, and as we do, we cultivate greater understanding.

Understanding will never be a glut on the market of interpersonal relations.

29

Insight on the Subway

BIBLE READING: John 14:13-18

Use not vain repetitions (Matthew 6:7).

Peggy, a bank teller, sat intrigued at what she was seeing across the aisle from her in the subway. Seemingly oblivious to anyone around her, a woman diligently fingered her rosary as her lips moved silently. Until the woman got off the train, Peggy's thoughts were occupied with, *What in the world does she hope to gain by all that 'bead saying'? Is that really praying?*

At times we do well to pause and give serious consideration to those things with which we may be all too familiar. We might ask ourselves such questions as, What makes a Christian's prayer unique? Why do we have the assurance that God hears *our* prayers? In there a Christian formula for prayer, and if so, what is it?

It was later the same day that Peggy's mind reverted to the subway incident. In need of certain supplies for the job, she asked the head of her department for them. The reply was a crisp, "Where is your requisition slip?" (The tone connoted, "You get nothing without a signed request)."

Peggy complied with the requirements and soon had the needed items. Meanwhile, she had begun to draw her own analogy: *My request was not granted because I didn't go through the right channels, didn't obtain the right signature. When I reversed the procedure, applied in the right place for the correct signature, presto—request granted!*

As she worked this out for herself, in a flash the Holy Spirit showed her the great spiritual principle of prayer *in the name of Jesus,* that asking "In His name" is the key. Not repetition, but simple faith that *Jesus* is the key to God's answering our prayer.

What about when we fail to ask in Jesus' name? Can we liken this to our dropping a letter in the mailbox without first affixing the required postage stamp? *That* letter is not going anyplace.

How sad that around the world millions are chanting their prayers, turning their prayer wheels, saying their beads. But, lacking the "stamp" of the name of Jesus, these prayers are not ascending to heaven; they're not going anyplace.

Sometimes it's in the daily business of living—like riding a subway to work—that God speaks to us and enlightens our understanding of the dire spiritual plight of those who do not know His Son, our Saviour, and who cannot, therefore, pray in His name.

30

Dumb Questions or Dumb Mistakes

BIBLE READING: James 1:1-6

She attended unto the things which were spoken
(Acts 16:14).

When we ask questions, what are we revealing: our ignorance, or the fact that we are smart?

Sue, in a trainee program for a new job, felt that asking
questions of the instructor would make her seem "dumb,"
so she kept quiet. But, noticing her unasked question, the
instructor encouraged her to speak up.

"But it's such a *dumb* question," Sue countered.

"Never mind about that. Don't be afraid to ask. Dumb
questions are easier to handle than dumb mistakes," the instructor insisted.

This should be an encouragement to all of us who hesi-
tate at times to ask when we don't know. It's also a scriptural position to take.

"If any of you lack wisdom, let him [her] ask of God"
(James 1:5).

God doesn't put us down for asking dumb questions; the
Lord bids us ask. The answers are available, so why should
we make dumb mistakes?

Asking is admitting, "I don't know it all." It takes a humble spirit to be willing to ask questions that might indeed make us appear ignorant in a certain area. But the result is well worth it.

God is interested in our questions. In fact, the road to wisdom is paved with questions, when they are asked of the right person. Think of the first Gentile convert in Europe, Lydia (a businesswoman, by the way). How many questions do you suppose she asked? She "attended" to what Paul was saying, so we can be sure she intercepted him to have her questions answered. The result? She had started out as a non-Christian businesswoman that Sabbath morning to worship; she returned home a convert to Christianity. And, her questions to life's greatest question settled, she is known wherever the Bible is read throughout the whole world.

31

The Importance of Doing Nothing

BIBLE READING: Psalm 23

In quietness and in confidence shall be your strength
(Isaiah 30:15).

Doing nothing. How could that possibly be important?
To those who have grown up in an atmosphere permeated
by a thick overlay of the Victorian work ethic, the idea that
doing nothing can have value will savor of outright heresy.

Nevertheless, we are not just hands and feet and tongue,
to keep on doing and going and talking. God has so consti-
tuted us that we need rest stops if we are going to be at our
best. Not a rest in order to do something else; rather, we
need time to do nothing so that our soul can catch up with
our body.

If you are like me, you find that it takes real discipline to
stop working once in a while. We've been programmed to
feel, *If I'm not busy, I'm wasting my time.* All too often as
children we were called on to explain if, for example, we
were just looking out the window.

"What are you doing?" Mother inquired, and our answer,
"Oh, nothing," sent her scurrying to find something con-

structive for us to do. Mom herself had not been permitted the luxury of doing nothing as a child, and she was just continuing the pattern.

What happens when we do take time into our own hands, even briefly? Generally we come back to our work with a freshness, a renewed spirit.

In my own experience, I find such times are vital to creativity. We cannot shut off our minds as though they were dictating machines. But we can consciously shut out the "oughts" and the "shoulds," and luxuriate in not being driven by anything or anyone for at least a few minutes. It's then that God can speak to the inner being. Call it meditating, if you will. God has always been for meditation (this generation didn't invent or discover it).

What did David do in the green pastures by the still waters? He restored his soul; rather, He let God restore his soul. And God is still in the soul-restoring business, if we will give ourselves permission to do nothing, and let Him heal and refresh and renew us periodically.

32

Criticism—Who Needs It?

BIBLE READING: Colossians 3:14-17

Love covers a multitude of sins (1 Peter 4:8, NASB).

Nobody likes to be criticized. And yet, need criticism always be a bad thing? No. Some people are willing to pay a high price for criticism. The position of critic in the world of the arts is a prestige job, carrying almost awesome power. In a very real sense, the professional critic can make or break an artist, musician, or author with his incisive evaluations.

On the happier side, genuine criticism offered in an acceptable manner can help make a success out of someone who would otherwise have remained mediocre and unfulfilled. In fact, constructive criticism is a vital aid to growth. Without valid critiquing from others, we might never know the discontent with our efforts that spurs us on to do better.

It's the *destructive* criticism that hurts. For we generally hear the critic as criticizing *us,* not *our work*—and we feel wounded all over.

Such destructive criticism shoots us down, frequently dulling the edge of whatever ability we have. It may cause us to mistrust ourselves in many areas of life.

We should examine our *motive* in offering any kind or

degree of criticism. "It's for your own good," is sometimes not true at all, and is usually best left unspoken. If we would honestly seek to develop the art of acceptable criticism, we need look no further than Matthew 7:12: "All things whatsoever ye would that men should do to you, do ye even so to them."

Marcia, a saleswoman, must never have given this a thought. She greeted an associate with, "Where in the world did you find a dress like *that,* Sue?" Inherent in her question was, "You have dreadful taste; *I* wouldn't be caught dead in a thing like that!"

By contrast, Joan noticed on the elevator an older woman who had some straggly hair. As they stepped off together, Joan said, "Here, let me fix your hair a little." She fussed with it a few seconds then stepped back and remarked, "There, now it looks just beautiful," and they smiled at each other. But what if Joan had cut the older woman down by saying, "Your hair looks *awful.* Don't you ever look in a mirror before you come to work?"

Love covers a multitude of shortcomings. If, therefore, you feel you must offer some criticism, it's always best to ask yourself, *Is it really for her own good? What is my motive? Am I sure she will see it as constructive?* It may then be all right to offer your criticism. But may I suggest that you do so in love, for love takes the sting out of criticism.

33

The Aura of Success

BIBLE READING: Luke 19:12-26

He commanded these servants to be called . . . that
he might know how much every man had gained
(v. 15).

Anne found it necessary to join the world of working
women after years of being a homemaker. Confiding her
fears and uncertainties to a friend, she asked, "Do you have
some advice for me?"

The friend thought for a minute and then said, "Yes.
Become good at something." She went on to explain:
"There's something about being successful at what you're
doing—a kind of aura. People tend to be willing to listen to
you, and they filter what you're saying through their concept that because you are successful, what you say is worth
hearing."

Our generation abounds with successful Christians: in the
arts, in business, in politics, in education—in practically
every area of life. These are persons who have "gotten good
at something," and other people have taken notice.

There's an often-repeated saying, "God has not called us
to be successful; He has called us to be faithful." Not for an

instant would I dispute the latter truth. But I would like to pose the question, How much is real success dependent on *faithfulness* to what one is doing? It's my thinking that God places no premium on mediocrity.

My son, Bruce, was visiting me. Being a writer himself, he had been using my typewriter. With a bit of a laugh he commented, referring to a little saying I have taped to my typing table, "That's quite a line, Mother." Then he quoted the saying, something I have heard Ethel Waters say a number of times: "God don't sponsor no flops."

I believe this. I don't really need to remind myself by the taped slip of paper. And believing it, I am personally interested in success as well as in faithfulness.

There are, obviously, material benefits for the person who is successful in her business or profession. But as Christians seeking first the Kingdom of God, we can look beyond the material and temporal, for there are also *spiritual* rewards. The greatest of these is the opportunity of obtaining a hearing when we witness to our faith in Christ. When we speak of God's guidance in our life, and it has apparently gotten us somewhere, our witness may be all the more credible to "the natural man [or woman who] receiveth not the things of the Spirit" (see 1 Corinthians 2:14). Some people will only heed those whom they view as "having made it."

Moreover, if the parable of the talents teaches anything, it is that God has success expectations. He is looking to us to use successfully those talents with which He has endowed us. Only then, according to the words of Jesus, will we hear His "Well done, thou good and faithful servant" (Matthew 25:21).

So it pays great dividends when we assess our abilities and then become good at something. Wouldn't you agree?

34

Living with Needless Frustration

BIBLE READING: John 21:15-22

What is that to you? (v. 20b)

Mary is a Christian. But she lives in sheer frustration five days a week on the job. What is her problem? She concerns herself far too much with what her colleagues do, how they perform at their work. She sees herself as much more conscientious than they. She dwells on what they should (in her opinion) be doing. And she would love to jump in and straighten out their attitudes toward their work.

Yet this is none of Mary's business.

Unless she can sort out what is and what is not her responsibility, she may well go on suffering all her working days from this kind of canker sore.

Such an attitude toward one's own job and those associated with it is not uncommon. Nor is it limited to our times. The Lord Jesus had to deal with it at times, even in His inner circle. We can't know all that went on among the disciples during those three and a half years. They were human, and doubtless their interpersonal relations were not all that might have been desired. But the gospels do give us some insight.

The day came when Jesus recommissioned Peter by the Sea of Galilee. Immediately after, Peter noticed John. Apparently it was common knowledge that John was especially close to Jesus, so Peter tested the Lord. It was as if he were saying, "Now that You've told *me* what I'm to do, how about John? What are You assigning to *him?*"

Christ's reply indicates that He read Peter's thoughts. His reply was in effect, "Never mind about John and what he should do, Peter. Just be sure *you* carry out *your* responsibilities."

As Christians, we have God's promise, "My grace is sufficient" (2 Corinthians 12:9). If we do our work as unto the Lord, He will give us the needed grace to tolerate the frustrations, whatever they are. We diminish our Christian witness when we fuss and fume about what the other person is supposed to be doing. Moreover, this savors of our setting ourselves up as judges. That's not for us; it's for the boss to judge! The Scripture is quite specific on this: "To his own master he standeth or falleth" (Romans 14:4).

Reminding ourselves of this truth can help keep us from daily frustration.

35

No Day for Grumbling

BIBLE READING: Philippians 2:12-16

Do all things without murmurings and disputings
(v. 14).

An old spiritual bemoans the fact that some people
"Grumble on a Monday, Tuesday, Wednesday. . . . Grumble
all the week through."

Unfortunately, it's more than a song.

Do we who belong to Christ have to be part of grumbling, murmuring, or arguing? If we are, how much different from the non-Christians around us does that make us?
Is this worth thinking about?

Grumbling might not be such unacceptable behavior if
it affected only the one who indulged in it. But that is
never so. And relationships are wrecked in the process.

The fact that others around us are having difficulty in
being compatible with one another is quite beside the point.
As God's people, we have a mandate to love our neighbor.
This allows no place or space for disputings. Living as we
do in a world that is hostile to all that we are taught by
Christ, we have our assignment from Him to shine as lights
in a dark world.

What are some of the ways we can "shine"?

One of the most effective is that we do not complain, murmur, or dispute when it would seem to an onlooker that that's the *only* thing to do. It takes a good degree of maturity and patience to hold our tongues. I've heard it described as "counting down rather than blasting off."

And what about the occasions when a complaint *is* in order? How do we handle that? Again, we can look to the Lord to keep us serene rather than uptight; to make us objective rather than subjective; to help us deal with specifics rather than generalities. Let me illustrate: Susan felt she had a legitimate complaint about her work situation. She might have made a griping session out of it after arranging an interview with her employer. But she chose not to. Instead, she calmly outlined the problem, not adding to it such inflammatory comments as, "Everything's wrong around here," or, "Nobody treats me right." She was specific and to the point. It's difficult to resolve vague, generalized complaints, no matter how willing the employer might be to rectify the situation. Also, by remaining calm and poised, we gain not only the attention but also the respect of the person who is in a position to effect needed change. Haranguing rarely accomplishes what we hope to see as a result of a valid complaint.

So it pays in our everyday working life, as in all situations, to determine that today is no day for grumbling. Surely this is the essence of Paul's counsel that we do all things without murmurings and disputings. Who can tell when, by our scriptural attitude, we might light a candle in our particular "dark world"?

36

The Message on the Freeway

BIBLE READING: Mark 1:32-35

In the morning will I direct my prayer unto thee (Psalm 5:3).

Frances had just picked up the third of her car-pool riders. As she started off again, she sighed and said, "What a morning! I sure hope things go better the rest of the day; they could hardly get any worse." Then, with the other women as empathetic listeners, she recited the frustrating happenings that had left her harried as she set off for work.

They were easing into the stream of freeway traffic when her eyes hit the big bold signs on the exit ramp: "WRONG WAY," and "DO NOT ENTER." *Funny,* she thought, *those signs must have been there before; wonder why I've never noticed them."*

"I should have seen signs like those before I got out of bed this morning," she said. "It might have warned me."

"Some mornings are like that," one of the women commented in an effort to comfort the driver.

It was later in the day that the thought struck Frances: *The signs—of course—God has His signs.* She began to ponder on God's right way to start her day if she would avoid total frustration. That morning she had just rushed into the day without a quiet moment with the Lord to give her serenity, *whatever the day brought.* From long experience, she knew better; she knew the peace and inner strength that come with that early appointment with God. Nevertheless, she had disregarded it—had "entered the wrong way" that morning.

For one reason or another, we all have such mornings, when things just do not go right. As Christians, we have recourse to never failing help. Also, we have the example of our Lord. With the demands of the day before Him, "rising up a great while before day, he went out" (Mark 1:35).

What does it really do for us in a practical way when, as has been poetically expressed, "we meet God in the morning when the day is at its best"?

In a very real sense, we are admitting, "Lord, I need You in my today. I know I can't be what You want me to be if I go it alone. If I do not turn my day over to You, I can't meet other people and treat them as I should, because only You can know what the day will bring." We rob ourselves when we enter the wrong way, not heeding the signs.

One of the Christian slogans of our day is, "Things go better with prayer." It's more than a trite saying; it is loaded with truth. Things *do* go better all day long when, like the psalmist, we direct our prayer to God in the morning.

37

Positive Peggy, Negative Nell

BIBLE READING: Romans 15:1-7

Whatsoever you do, do it heartily, as to the Lord
(Colossians 3:23).

Is it possible that we can do heartily, "as to the Lord,"
something that in no way glorifies Him?

Let me contrast two Christian women in the marketplace:

Peggy is a receptionist and one of the most popular young
women in her company. Nell, a typist with the same company—well, that's a different story.

If we could listen in on some of the comments about the
two Christians, it would go something like this:

"Peggy? Oh, there isn't a nicer girl in the place. She's so
friendly and helpful and cooperative. Sure, she's *religious,*
and she's quick to tell the rest of us what she believes. But
she's so thoughtful, and she's always cheerful. She's *good* for
people. We like Peggy."

Of Nell they would probably say, "Oh, she's all right, I
guess, if you like that kind of person. But she has such a
condemning attitude, and she preaches at us all the time.
Whatever we suggest doing, she's sure to say smugly, 'I'm a
Christian; I *don't* do that.' Some of us wonder if she majors
in negatives."

Which of the two is likely to make an impact for Christ?

It's been my observation that the world at large is never impressed with what we *don't* do. I am not advocating a go-along-with-everything policy. There are occasions when as Christians, we must take a stand, not only *for* but *against.* But—and again, I can only speak from my own observation—I find that when a Christian is warm and friendly and thoughtful and *happy,* non-Christians will respect what they view as our "religious foibles." We're then in a position to get them to listen when we explain what makes us what we are.

It's difficult—almost impossible—to get an unbeliever to be interested in what interests us if they don't like us. When the dislike is founded on our sometimes churlish attitudes in the name of Christianity, it will take some cultivating of a relationship before we can introduce the person to our loving and understanding Saviour.

It's an awesome thought that you and I may be the only reflection of Jesus that someone has. So what image are we projecting: one that's joyous and free and exciting and hopeful, or one that's clouded with *don'ts?*

Let's not settle for being a negative Nell when, with all the resources that are ours in Christ Jesus, we can be a positive Peggy.

38

Responsible Anticipation

BIBLE READING: 1 Thessalonians 4:14-18

I will come again (John 14:3).

God has different ways of bringing us to Himself. For me, hearing for the first time that Jesus Christ would come back to earth made me listen to a preacher who was about his Father's business at a Saturday night social gathering. Consequently, the teaching of the second coming has always been exciting truth to me.

Not long ago I was in a group where the topic surfaced, and one after another said, "The Lord can't come too soon to suit me; I'll be so glad to get out of this job!" The specifics were a little different in each case, but the message was loud and clear: The reason I want Jesus to return is that I will then be relieved of certain unpleasant things in this life.

Far be it from me to judge anyone else's motives, but these were all spelled out. This made me look into my own heart. What does it mean to me that Jesus is coming again?

Then I began to think of the words of the apostle John on this subject: "Every man that has this hope . . . purifies himself, even as he [Christ] is pure" (1 John 3:3).

How purifying is this blessed hope to most of us? If we knew that Jesus were coming tomorrow, what would you and I hastily clean up, or get rid of, in order to meet His scrutiny?

But we don't know when He will come. No one does.

But if we *could* know? What would be the thing you'd want most to be doing when Christ comes?

This brings to mind something from my childhood. My mother would sometimes go by train to the nearest city to shop. She would leave me a number of things, like dusting, or washing the dishes, to do while she was gone. As soon as she was out of sight, I would grab a book and sit down to read. Lost in my book, I would only come back to reality when the train whistled and I knew Mom would be home soon. I would fly around, trying to do what I should have been doing. But there was never time, and I was ashamed to face my mother. I had both disobeyed and disappointed her.

Jesus gave us something specific to do. His last words were, "You shall be witnesses unto me" (Acts 1:8).

When He comes He *will* relieve us of our problem situations, but He will also require an accounting of what we have been doing to win others to Him in His absence.

39

It Takes Two to Tattle

BIBLE READING: Proverbs 26:20-28

Where no wood is, there the fire goes out (v. 20).

The Bible is the most practical of books. While it lays no claims to be a manual on job ethics, it has a way of zeroing in on the real problems. For usually it's not so much the facilities or the equipment or the work itself that cause us frustration; it's the human element, including our own behavior.

Among the greatest troublemakers, without a doubt, is the talebearer; and the Bible has a lot to say about such a person.

Why does a person revel in tattling on a fellow worker?

Frequently it's not from vicious intent; rather, she has found that by having a gossip "scoop" she can be the center of attention, at least temporarily. Sally, a new Christian, had been guilty of gossip. And, she had found that, as Solomon wrote, "The words of a gossip are tempting morsels" (Proverbs 18:8, Berkeley). For a while after her conversion she continued to bask in the attention she got. But the Holy Spirit began to convict her as she read, "Let the words of my mouth . . . be acceptable in thy sight" (Psalm 19:14). Sally asked forgiveness from God, and grace to overcome her noxious habit.

Not only does our gossiping grieve the Lord, it ultimately loses us friends. A little thought would reveal to us that a true friend is not gained by such slimy methods as tale-bearing about other people (for who will be the next victim?).

It takes more than recognition and determination, however, to shake this detestable practice. We may have to look deep within ourselves and ask, Why do I indulge in gossip? What do I hope to gain by it? Am I using tales to knock someone down in the hope of thus upping my own image in my crowd?

It takes sincere prayer and dependence on the Holy Spirit; it calls for daily watchfulness and obedience to the Scripture that bids me, "Keep thy tongue from evil, and thy lips from speaking guile" (Psalm 34:13).

A simple, preventive guideline for implementing that verse is asking ourselves:

1. Is what I'm about to say *true?*
2. Is it any of my business to spread it abroad?
3. Am I being kind in telling it?

The Bible is clear that it takes two to gossip: the listener plays her part. "An evildoer listens to wicked lips" (Proverbs 17:4, NASB).

Without a ready listener, the gossipy person can be likened to a fire that dies out when the fuel is not replenished. But words once spoken can never be unspoken. As James, speaking of the tongue, warns us, "How great a matter a little fire kindleth" (James 3:5).

It may be a problem to avoid listening to talebearing; we may alienate the one who feels she just has to tell us something "she doesn't want anyone else to hear" (a clue that it's probably gossip). But, apart from not partaking in something which the Bible condemns, in the end we will be helping the person. As she gains insight into the negative use of the tongue, she can be helped to see the positive aspects. Again in the practical book of Proverbs, we find this salutary comment: "She opens her mouth in wisdom" (31:26, NASB).

No place there for gossip—and no gossip to listen to.

40

Don't Turn down that Compliment

BIBLE READING: Philippians 4:9-13

A word fitly spoken is like apples of gold in pictures of silver (Proverbs 25:11).

Have you ever paid a sincere compliment to a friend, only to have her look a little uncomfortable and say, "Oh, it was nothing."

It may be that the friend had just done something especially well, or you had heard something nice about her and had passed it on. Whatever the occasion, she had not seemingly been able to accept your sincere compliment.

Usually there are reasons why we do what we do. It could be that in this woman's home, as she was growing up, no one ever complimented another; family members took each other for granted, or worse, they criticized one another. The result is that she has no background for accepting genuine praise for anything she does or is. In fact, a compliment is something of an embarrassment to her.

A saleswoman, Phyllis, had this problem. Her supervisor was pleased with Phyllis's work and told her so. The response was disappointing: "Me—*my* work! It's not all that

95

good," Phyllis said. The supervisor paid little heed the first time, but when more than once this employee countered with negative statements, the supervisor said to herself, *All right. That's the last time I'll compliment her!* (And the decision may spill over to other employees also). None of us likes to feel she has said the wrong thing.

How can we respond to a compliment gracefully if this has never been a part of our way of life?

One way might be to accept it with a smile that speaks for you. Another response can be, "It makes me feel good to have you say that about me," or, "I'm so glad you noticed. Thank you for telling me." This way both of you are happy. The person giving the compliment is glad she did, and you are encouraged by the recognition that your work is pleasing.

The person who has difficulty in graciously accepting a compliment is usually hesitant about taking any kind of favor from another person. This attitude, in turn, robs someone of the joy of giving. The Bible says, "It is more blessed to give than to receive" (Acts 20:35b). But how can we know the joy and blessing of giving unless there is someone who is willing to receive? This is true even of a compliment, so why turn it down?

41

"You're Wrong" Says "I'm Right"

BIBLE READING: Romans 13:7-10

Love works no ill to [her] neighbour (v. 10).

The riders were all picked up, and the car-pool conversation turned to the subject of diet; in particular, the relative merits of instant breakfast foods.

Marilyn was voicing her views on nutrition when she was jumped on by Grace with, "You're *wrong.*" Grace then proceeded to hold forth on her own ideas. It was noticeable that she was not getting much of a hearing.

This woman was probably unaware of the import of her words, "You're wrong"; quite likely she had said the same thing many times, never realizing that in declaring the other person wrong she was in effect saying, "I'm right."

Some people seem to have an overriding compulsion to be proven right. They can't tolerate it that anyone should think they just might not be right 100 percent of the time. But this attitude spells doom to good relationships.

To be sure, Miss or Mrs. Right doesn't necessarily mean to convey that *you* are wrong; rather, she has in mind, "What you *said* is wrong," or "You're *doing* it the wrong way." But that's not how it comes out. The inference can only be that "I am right," not, "There's a better way to do it," or, "Your information may not be correct."

The sad part is that so often two or three people will get into an argument over some relatively unimportant issue. To illustrate: someone in the course of conversation says, "It was a Friday—" But she is cut short by someone else insisting, "No. You're *wrong*. It was a *Tuesday*—" Since the event, whatever it was, is in the past, who cares which day it was? What difference can it make? More importantly, is it worth wrecking relationships over?

How much better to heed the injunction to work no ill to our neighbor.

Has it occurred to you that the Lord Jesus could have been right every time? He could have put down almost everybody with whom He came in contact by saying, "You're wrong." But our Lord didn't *have* to be recognized as right; He was not on an ego trip. He could allow Himself the triumph of letting other people's feelings be important to Him.

We, on our finite level, can know something of this quiet inner triumph. It's a good feeling when we let ourselves refrain from proving "I'm right," with its tacit, "You're wrong."

It will always be right to stand for what we know to be spiritually and morally invariable.

Being right in order to prove someone else wrong is a hollow victory and a mark of immaturity as a Christian.

42

Living with What You Can't Change

BIBLE READING: Hebrews 13:5-8

His compassions fail not. They are new every morning: great is thy faithfulness (Lamentations 3:22*b*-23).

There is almost always something about our work environment or our associates that we would like to change. We feel that things would be more pleasant or that they would go more smoothly if only these changes could be made. Sometimes we can help to effect some ourselves. But what of the situations where seemingly nothing can be done?

Reinhold Niebuhr gave us a solution in what has come to be known as the "Serenity Prayer":

O God, give us serenity to accept what cannot be changed, courage to change what should be changed, and wisdom to distinguish the one from the other.

This is as profound as it is simple. Inherent in the first thought is that we explore the possibilities for change (how else would we conclude that nothing can be done?) and ask the Lord to give us what it takes to live with what we cannot change. Calmness of spirit, serenity, is possible even when we recognize that it's futile to attempt changes.

What can give us this kind of peace of heart? What can make the workday tolerable? One thing—and it's a very down-to-earth truth—is the certain knowledge that five o'clock will come. Though we cannot change the situation, we can leave it when we leave the building. An attitude of "This too shall pass" can make anything tolerable. You may have heard of the Christian who habitually gave as his favorite verse, "And it came to pass." As he viewed his circumstances, *whatever* they were, they were not eternal; they would pass.

For our comfort, whatever the burden of our lot, we have God's sure promise, *"As thy days, so shall thy strength be"* (Deuteronomy 33:25, italics added).

Because this strength comes from God, it can extend even to enabling us to live with what we cannot change.

43

You Can Love Yourself

BIBLE READING: Luke 10:25-28

Thou shalt love thy neighbour as thyself (Matthew 19:19).

Much is being said, and perhaps even more written, about loving ourselves. And many people are confused.

Doesn't the Bible teach humility? Aren't we exhorted not to think of ourselves more highly than we ought (Romans 12:3)?

Yet was it not our Lord Himself who instructed us to love our neighbor as ourselves? Obviously, then, we should love ourselves.

Both schools of thought are scriptural. How, then, can we reconcile the seeming contradiction?

What if, in our bid for humility, we do not properly love ourselves? How then will we love our neighbor? What measure of love will we have to give others?

Jesus never gave a commandment (1) that we *could* not keep; (2) that we *should* not keep.

In striving to love our neighbor, we need to consider this aspect: it is a fact of life that we view other people with the same glasses through which we see ourselves. If I view myself as not worth much, not very important to anyone, I am likely to view the people with whom I associate in the same light.

Why is it possible for you and me to love ourselves?

Is it because of who we are—our name or position, talents or intellect, personality traits or whatever? No. We can love or esteem ourselves because of who we are *in Christ.*

We are *valuable* to God. We are His purchased possession, bought not with silver and gold (for there isn't enough in all the world to redeem you or me!).

We are "accepted in the beloved" (Ephesians 1:6), accepted *as we are.* God does not ask us to change first: to lose ten pounds, to memorize twenty-five Bible verses, to shape up and then apply for salvation. No, He *"loved* us, and *washed* us from our sins" (Revelation 1:5, italics added)—in that order.

And these are just a few of the reasons why we can love ourselves.

When we appropriate God's good things for ourselves, we can then begin to accept our "neighbors" *as they are,* and begin to love them.

We *can* have a high view of ourselves—without "thinking too highly."

We *can* love ourselves. And this will be reflected in our relationships with those around us.

44

But It Isn't Fair!

BIBLE READING: 1 John 2:24-29

He which hath begun a good work in you will perform it (Philippians 1:6).

Carol had waited expectantly for the day when she would be promoted. She had worked hard, trying her best to be cooperative and pleasant with her colleagues; she had taken courses to expand her knowledge and improve her performance on the job. She felt she had proven herself to her employer and that she deserved a promotion.

The day came. She was called into the boss's office, and walking on air, she obeyed the summons.

Moments later she emerged. Her head down, the spring gone from her step, she made her way back to her desk. The company was transferring an employee from another branch; she would fill the position which Carol had so confidently expected would be hers.

"It isn't *fair,*" she said to herself, and her colleagues agreed with her. "How can they do such a thing? You're the one who should get the promotion," they insisted as they attempted to console Carol. Their intent was good, but their words just served to make her feel more hurt, more bitter, to reinforce her feelings that she had been treated shabbily by the company she had served loyally.

This is not an uncommon occurrence in the business world, as we all know. It's good, then, to be prepared to cope with it and to have some means to help someone who has this shattering experience. It's also a good opportunity for us as Christians to evaluate how to react to situations. Are we *really* any different from the non-Christian at such times? Should we be?

We're all human and vulnerable to hurt and disappointment. But it's not what happens to us that is all-important; it's what we let happenings do to us that marks us as God's people. Suppose, for instance, that Carol, after a day or so of brooding, had decided, "I'm a Christian. I belong to the Lord. *He is sovereign* in my life; *Christ,* not the boss, is in charge." The whole picture would have changed.

I know of such an instance. By accepting the company's edict as a part of God's plan for her life, a young woman, although she suffered some disappointment, nevertheless found that God had a whole new sphere for her where she could serve Him as she never had been able to before. Ultimately she rose higher on the job than she had ever anticipated. Sometimes, all unwittingly, the boss is just furthering God's plan for our life. God will not treat us unfairly.

> For I know the plans I have for you, says the LORD. They are plans for good and not for evil, to give you a future and a hope (Jeremiah 29:11, TLB).

It makes for happiness when we look for *God's* hand in our circumstances.

45

The Oughts and the Shoulds

BIBLE READING: Deuteronomy 10:11-13

What doth the LORD thy God require of thee . . . ?
(vv. 12-13).

"I don't really want to, but I feel I should." How often
we hear this from people who appear to be able to determine their own conduct.

Are you one of these, a victim of "the shoulds"? Do you
find yourself drawn into doing things you would rather not
do?

What can one do at such a point? First, it would be well
to pause and consider, What is the "should" related to?
Who or what is the force compelling me to do it, or to feel
guilty for not doing it? Second, we need to question, Is this
compulsion in line with what *God* requires of me?

In today's reading, God has spelled out His requirements
for us quite specifically. We are:

1. to fear (reverence) Him
2. to walk in all His ways
3. to love and serve Him with our whole heart and soul
   and mind

4. to keep His commandments and statutes

It's worthy of noting that God's requirements for us are given for our good (v. 13*b*). Can we apply this test to the shoulds and oughts that others impose upon us?

And if not?

What happens when we submit because we feel we have to, no matter how unwilling we are? Usually we feel tension, resentment, and other negative emotions toward the person or the situation that has placed us under the "tyranny of the ought."

Let me make it quite clear, however, that I am in no way advocating that we be irresponsible or careless regarding our duty toward our colleagues and other people. We cannot fulfill God's requirements as stated without having right attitudes toward those around us. I am saying that we need to analyze the shoulds and oughts that tend to drive us. It was never God's intention that we be tyrannized but that we should experience His peace as we seek to meet *His* requirements for us.

You may want to give some thought to this concept the next time you are unreasonably compelled to do something because you feel you *should.*

46

Jealousy, the Self-Defeating Emotion

BIBLE READING: Galatians 5:19-26

Let us not be desirous of vain glory, provoking one
another, envying one another (v. 26).

Marty, a popular office manager, was complimented by a
colleague on her latest promotion. "But why are you always
so interested in the people on the lower rungs?" the friend
questioned.

With a smile, Marty answered, "I like people." Then she
added, "When I received my first small promotion, I learned
something. It was this: if I had not been there and prepared,
the woman above me might not have gotten the promotion
she did. So I began to take an interest in the person under
me and to train her. My reasoning was that if another position above mine became vacant, I didn't want to miss the
opportunity to slip in there just because there was no one
ready to step into my shoes."

For either the Christian or the non-Christian, this makes
sense. The opposite point of view is, Why should I bother
to help someone else up the ladder? And frequently this
attitude is nourished by a spirit of jealousy. The Bible warns

against such a trait, describing jealousy as "cruel as the grave" (Song of Solomon 8:6). The New Testament—calling jealousy *envy*—rates it among the "works of the flesh" (Galatians 5:19-21).

While it may exhibit itself in an unwillingness to help someone else, jealousy is really self-defeating. The sure antidote to this negative emotion is found in Romans 12:15a: "Rejoice with them that do rejoice." The enjoyment of another person's good fortune, recognition of ability, or any other cause for rejoicing, makes it yours as well as hers. Jealousy builds walls shutting out friendship; rejoicing in another's joy can tear these walls down and, in their place, build bridges to good relationships.

How worthwhile and satisfying it is to look down a rung or two of the ladder of success and see, not too far behind us, someone we have helped and encouraged along the way. There's nothing self-defeating about that!

47

The T. G. I. F. Club

BIBLE READING: Romans 14:5-8

He that regardeth the day, regardeth it unto the Lord (v. 6).

A friend of mine has on a shelf in her office one of the most appealing animal pictures I have ever seen. It portrays a kitten with a world of expression on its face saying, "Is it FRIDAY yet?" It's an amusing picture, and my friend assures me it never fails to evoke comments such as, "That's how I feel, too."

Friday. What is it about our job that makes Friday such a pinnacle day? I even saw a lapel button glorifying this day, with its T.G.I.F.—"Thank God It's Friday."

It might be worth considering some of the ramifications of this statement, however lightly spoken. Seemingly there is a T.G.I.F. club, a group of people who live for Friday from the time they open the door to their place of employment on Monday morning. True, we all fall prey to weariness; also, we are the victims of our circumstances and of the expectations of employers and associates. There are days when even the most loyal and devoted employee wishes for a day off, or that the alarm clock would never ring. This, however, is different from being a chronic Friday watcher.

What does God's Word say about our day—any day, every day? "This is the day which the LORD hath made; we will rejoice and be glad in it" (Psalm 118:24).

This day (today) be it Monday, Tuesday, Wednesday, Thursday, Saturday, Sunday—or Friday—is the day God has made.

It's easy for us to glibly quote this verse from the Psalms, and sometimes it is the very worst thing we can say to someone. The person who expresses a wish that Friday would come may be laboring under stress we know nothing about; she may be carrying a burden she cannot share with us, so we need to ask God to make us sensitive to how we toss Bible verses around.

For *ourselves,* however, we can determine that each day has worth for itself, that Monday is not just a stepping-stone to Friday (and freedom from the job).

It interests me that the verse reads, "I will be glad and rejoice." Note the "I will." Rejoicing and being glad day after day may often call for an act of the will, a deliberate choosing to rejoice rather than to adopt a negative attitude. Both positive and negative attitudes tend to rub off on those around us. We do *not* live unto ourselves (see Romans 14:7). We can, then, by accepting each day for itself and rejoicing in it, help other people toward this happy and satisfying way of life.

After all, this day is the only day that is ours for certain. Why should we spoil it by fruitless wishing for Friday?

48

A Great Way to Keep Christ's Law

BIBLE READING: Galatians 6:1-5

Whenever we can we should always be kind (v. 10, TLB).

An editor friend in a publishing house has a way of going the extra mile in offering help. Rather than the more usual, "Can we help you?" she asks, *"How* can we help you?" (The inference is that it's a foregone conclusion that she is going to help.) She wants to know how to be most effective in her help.

How vastly different from, "Why should I help you? I have enough work of my own to do."

True, each of us has responsibilities. But must this fact conflict with the scriptural injunction to bear one another's burdens? Where a right, an emotionally healthy, attitude prevails, we can manage to cope with our work and still be considerate of our fellow employees. It usually doesn't take much time to do little kindnesses. And since we're all human and fallible, the bread of kindness that we cast on the waters may come back to us just when we need it most. Moreover, we will be keeping God's Law.

"But I'm not under Law; I'm under grace," you may be

countering in your mind. This, too, is true. But should grace be less gracious than Law? Less understanding of another's need for a helping hand?

If you are of a logical turn of mind, you may also have to hurdle the verse that bids us to bear our own burden (Galatians 6:5). How can we bear one another's burdens without negating "every man shall bear his own burden"? One thing we can be sure of is that the Bible does not contradict itself. Without going into the theological ramifications, a simple solution would seem to be this: the one who is dutifully bearing his own burden will, nevertheless, welcome a little help from time to time. Wouldn't you or I? And this does not disqualify us from bearing our own burden; it just eases it for us a little.

Ultimately, none of us is asked to be her own burden bearer, unless she *chooses* to be. Christ's loving invitation to us is "Come unto me, all ye that labour and are heavy laden, and I will give you rest" (Matthew 11:28).

It is as we accept this invitation and take our burdens to the Lord and leave them there, that we return to the job rested and relaxed. We then are enabled to say to a more weary person, "How can I help you?"

Can you think of a more satisfying way of fulfilling the law of Christ (see Romans 13:10)?

49

That's My Cross, I Guess

BIBLE READING: John 15:18-22

If any man will come after me, let him . . . take up
his cross, and follow me (Matthew 16:24).

It was "one of those mornings"; nothing went right.
Either the alarm failed to go off, or Jean failed to hear it;
the car took forever to start; a stalled vehicle on the high-
way further delayed her. Moreover, she'd had to leave without breakfast. When she finally arrived at work, the same
gremlin seemed to have pursued her. The typewriter acted
up. There was no response to her call for a service man.
And to top it all, the coffee machine was out of order!

Oh well, she sighed, *I guess that's just my cross,* and she
resigned herself as best she could to bear the rest of the
day.

Most of us can readily identify with Jean's frustrations.
Who hasn't experienced such mornings? But a cross!

If such things as traffic jams, unreliable alarm clocks,
machines that don't work, inconveniences, and delays are
"crosses to be borne," then the whole world can be said to
be cross-bearers at some time or other. The non-Christian

burns her toast, and misses her bus or train; her car has flat tires, she runs out of gas, she has to contend with uncooperative service men, and so forth. But can any one of these irritations, or even a combination of them in one day, be properly called "my cross"? Not in the sense in which our Lord meant it when He said, "If any man will come after me, let him deny himself, and take up his cross, and follow me" (Matthew 16:24).

What, then, is this cross?

This raises the question, For what was Jesus crucified?

Was it not for asserting His relationship to God the Father, for declaring Himself to be the *Son of God?*

For this, the self-righteous people of His day hated Jesus; they demanded His crucifixion.

The world's standards have never changed in this respect. Even though most of us in our favored circumstances know little or nothing of persecution for our faith, for asserting that we are the children of God through faith in His Son, who died for us, at times we can still sense the world's hatred. In fact, if we never suffer some kind of ridicule or sneering, we may do well to question whether we are any kind of a Christian witness at all.

In essence, then, a cross is something we bear for Christ, for identifying ourselves with Him and with His people and with the Bible's standards in a day of moral decay and spiritual confusion.

Thinking this over may cause us to question, as does a hymn writer, "Must Jesus bear the cross alone?"

50

Formula, the Golden Rule

BIBLE READING: Romans 12:10-18

As much as lieth in you, live peaceably (v. 18).

You are a saleswoman, and you have your own share of irritating situations with customers. It may be their impatience, their unreasonable expectations or demands, or even their downright rudeness to you. Most of all you become upset over being treated by the customer as though you were a thing rather than the person you are.

By the very nature of things, however, a salesperson is also a *customer* dealing with people on the other side of the counter.

What can you as a saleswoman learn by being a customer?

It pays when we put ourselves in the other person's shoes. It may be that you can freshly assess your own attitudes. This is valuable in that people generally *re*act to how we act.

To be sure, there will always be those who, for one reason or another, never respond positively to anything or anybody. They seem to be programmed on a negative disk: they dislike the merchandise, they gripe about the service, they're suspicious about every transaction, and in general, it's impossible to please them.

Paul may have had such people in mind when he suggested, "As much as lieth in you, live peaceably with all men" (Romans 12:18). But how to do this? Would the Golden Rule (Matthew 7:12) be the formula?

Nothing is more conciliatory than a warm smile. This has been called "the shortest distance between two people," and a smile doesn't cost a penny nor take up our time.

Another tactic is to listen to the customer without interrupting, even if it is "the same old story." I know a woman who works part time in a large department store. She has such a way with the customers, especially the older, often lonely, and neglected ones, that many of them shop only on the days they know she will be there.

But isn't it wasting the company's time, listening to people? you may be asking. Not when you are generating goodwill for the company!

Again, you may question, Why should I put myself out to please people who are difficult?

Why? Because in doing so you will be following the scriptural injunction to "live peaceably." If you feel that your own resources are not enough, what better way to prove Philippians 4:13: "I can do all things through Christ which strengtheneth me."

Here is the enabling to follow the Golden Rule.

51

Call Your Administrator

BIBLE READING: Jeremiah 33:1-3

God said, Let there be light: and there was light
(Genesis 1:3).

We live in an awesome world of computers. While I'm
not one to bow down and worship this marvel of man's
God-given brain, I must admit that I'm intrigued at times
with the spiritual analogies the computer suggests.

One day I heard some people discussing how the computer
"talks back" to them.

"What does it say?" I asked.

The ready reply was "Well, for one thing, when something goes wrong it spells out, 'Stop! Call your systems
administrator.'"

Knowing my ignorance of the area, the top man in the
company explained a little further. Instantly the analogy
was obvious.

When in trouble, on whom should we call? *Our* "systems Administrator"!

Who is this mighty Authority who has all the answers,
who can rectify all the errors and set us off again on a right
course?

Who but *God?* With His voice He threw the stars into place. Four words—and deep darkness turned into light. Seven more words, "Let us make man in our image"—and man, the creator of the most sophisticated computers, was created.

Doesn't it make sense, then, that when in the course of the day we run into problems of any kind we stop and call for our systems Administrator?

In God's printout we have His eternal promise: "Call to Me, and I will answer you, and I will tell you great and mighty things, which you do not know" (Jeremiah 33:3, NASB). Nor is there ever the qualification of "If I can," or "If it's convenient."

It's comforting also to realize that any of us can call upon the divine Administrator. This is not necessarily so in the world of the computer. I understand that there are levels of trust and responsibility; lesser operators do not have access to the top systems administrator. Here the spiritual analogy breaks down, for "God is no respecter of persons" (Acts 10:34). His ear is ever open to our cry, no matter who we are or what our position on the employee scale.

One thing that would keep us from enjoying the privileges that are ours, is if we prefer to "go it alone."

Suppose the trained computer operator decided, when things went awry, "I can handle it." What then? She would be stymied, stuck with a sophisticated piece of equipment that just stalled.

I'm reminded of what a scientist told me some years ago: "A computer is nothing of itself. It's so stupid that it cannot by itself discern between a comma and the key word in a sentence; when something goes wrong, it grinds to a halt and screams for an operator."

Nothing has changed in that respect, except the terminology now is, "Stop! Call for your systems administrator." The sensible operator does just that.

We, too, if we're smart, will recognize our own limitations, and when we need help *we* will stop and call for our systems Administrator.

52

Truth and Love Can Meet

BIBLE READING: Zechariah 8:16-19

Speaking the truth in love (Ephesians 4:15).

"I can't stand Grace's patronizing attitude," a junior clerk complained to a friend in her office.

"Why don't you go to her and talk it over?" the friend suggested.

"Oh, she'd never listen" was Grace's reply. "And besides, I'm a Christian."

Why should we infer that Christianity and openness can never meet?

It's an encouraging indication for better relationships that in today's society there is more emphasis on honest communication. For too long, it seems to me, there was a tacit "peace at any price" understanding in Christian circles. But, things being what they are and all of us being human, occasions occur when we need to air our grievances.

For example, Mary Ann is the managing type. No matter which department she's in or for however short a time, she wants to take over. All the while resentment is brewing in a number of the other employees. But it's a Christian organization, and the staff has been imbued with the concept that it's better to keep quiet than to risk rocking the boat (even though this might lead to calming the waters permanently).

In such situations neither the truth nor a Christian attitude need be sacrificed; these are not mutually exclusive. The Bible counsels us to speak the truth in love. In fact, this is a mark of growing in Christ, as the whole verse indicates (Ephesians 4:15).

Speaking the truth can often clear the air; speaking in love will soften the explanation. The fact that we are obeying God's injunction in seeking to correct a situation will generally bring its own good results.

Sandra, a businesswoman, was concerned over her growing ill feelings toward an associate at work. After praying about it, she reminded the Lord that He had promised to give wisdom to those who ask Him for it. Buoyed up by the fact that she was taking the scriptural route, she approached her associate and told her how she felt; she did "speak the truth in love." The two discussed the problem, and although Sandra had been somewhat apprehensive, she left the other woman's presence happier than she had been for weeks.

"Only someone who cares would have bothered to come and explain to me so lovingly," the woman said, "and I'll watch that trait from now on. I'll always thank you for coming to me as you did."

Not always will the outcome be so gratifying and the results so speedy. But it will always be right to do the right thing in the right way and to "speak the truth in love."

Moody Press, a ministry of the Moody Bible Institute, is designed for education, evangelization and edification. If we may assist you in knowing more about Christ and the Christian life, please write us without obligation to: Moody Press, c/o MLM, Chicago, Illinois 60610.